COMING INTO
EIGHTY

Books by May Sarton

Poetry

Encounter in April
Inner Landscape
The Lion and the Rose
The Land of Silence
In Time Like Air
Cloud, Stone, Sun, Vine
A Private Mythology
As Does New Hampshire
A Grain of Mustard Seed
A Durable Fire
Collected Poems, 1930–1973
Selected Poems of May Sarton
(edited by Serena Sue Hilsinger and Lois Byrnes)
Halfway to Silence
Letters from Maine
The Silence Now
Collected Poems 1930–1993

Novels

The Single Hound
The Bridge of Years
Shadow of a Man
A Shower of Summer Days
Faithful Are the Wounds
The Birth of a Grandfather
The Fur Person
The Small Room
Joanna and Ulysses

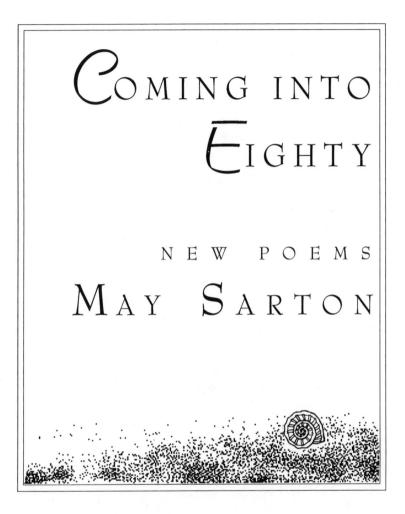

COMING INTO EIGHTY

NEW POEMS

MAY SARTON

W·W·NORTON & COMPANY·NEW YORK·LONDON

Acknowledgments

Some of these poems originally appeared in
The Café Review, Home, Opera News, Paris Review,
and *Poetry.*

The text of this book is composed in Cochin,
with the display set in Bernhard Modern.
Composition by Maple-Vail Composition Services.
Manufacturing by The Courier Companies, Inc.
Book design by Antonina Krass.

Library of Congress Cataloging-in-Publication Data
Sarton, May, 1912–
Coming into eighty : new poems / May Sarton.
p. cm.
I. Title.
PS3537.A832C66   1994
811'.52 — dc20   94-18659

ISBN 0-393-03689-8

W. W. Norton & Company, Inc.
500 Fifth Avenue, New York, N.Y. 10110
W. W. Norton & Company Ltd.
10 Coptic Street, London WC1A 1PU

1 2 3 4 5 6 7 8 9 0

To Pierrot
The Muse Mews

CONTENTS

9

I have loved W. B. Yeats for many reasons, not least because he changed his style radically in old age, writing perhaps his greatest poems after the age of eighty. I hoped I might be able to do the same, though I did not imagine I would live to be eighty since both my parents died at seventy, five years apart.

But here I am, willy nilly, writing poems in my seventy-ninth and eightieth years, and the reason is partly because I am a foreigner in the land of old age and have tried to learn its language.

These poems are minimal because my life is reduced to essences. No more travel except across a room, dictating instead of writing a journal, a lot of meditating, looks at the sea from my window down at the end of the long field, and as always I am mesmerized by flowers on the table beside me. I live with essences, with what is innermost these days because what is outermost is often beyond my strength. I can pay that absolute attention Simone Weil has called "prayer" to a bird at the feeder outside my window or a bunch of anemones opening to show purple hearts. I have more time for being and less ability to do than ever before. So a poem that flies in in the middle of the night is very acceptable — and in this book the poems did actually fly in on the cold air as I opened the door for Pierrot in the middle of the night.

These poems are dedicated to Pierrot, my Himalayan cat,

a bluepoint with blue-gray head, paws, and tail, the rest of him an elegant cream color, his huge eyes sapphire blue. Between one and three every morning he woke me with imperious mews to be let in, so I had to get up, go down a steep flight of stairs, and unlock the heavy front door. By the time I got upstairs again I was wide awake, and these poems made their appearances, a new kind of poem for me. They came of their own free will and I had only to accept radical change and use it as best I could. Sometimes they astonished me, they were so unlike what I had written before. I jotted down a few lines and went back to sleep.

I did not realize until I began thinking about a preface that one reason these nights were so inspired was simply that, in my bedroom in the middle of the night, there were no telephone calls, no UPS knocking on the door. The silence was intoxicating. Even more important, I was separated from the devastating clutter on my desk one floor up. So, wide awake, with space and order around me, a purring Pierrot by my side, the poems were free to come as they did.

The next morning I brought the notes up to my desk and with very little changed from the spontaneous night writing, wrote the poems down.

I was extremely happy during that magical year.

Of course any experiment with form induces a lot of anxiety, so it was encouraging to receive *Poetry*'s Levinson Prize for a group published in their December issue of 1992. The *Paris Review* had also published three poems.

After several months Pierrot gave up his mews because a friend had created a cat door for him in the cellar. Now he comes and goes as he pleases and I sleep through the night.

Nevertheless there was a magic year when I was writing in a new form and perhaps it will happen again, because I can still escape all that entangles my imagination up here in my office. There is still the wonderful silence and freedom of two A.M. at Wild Knoll.

May Sarton
York, Maine

COMING INTO EIGHTY

Coming into eighty
I slow my ship down
For a safe landing.
It has been battered,
One sail torn, the rudder
Sometimes wobbly.
We are hardly a glorious sight.
It has been a long voyage
Through time, travail and triumph,
Eighty years
Of learning what to be
And how to become it.

One day the ship will decompose
and then what will become of me?
Only a breath
Gone into nothingness
Alone
Or a spirit of air and fire
Set free?
Who knows?

Greet us at landfall
The old ship and me,
But we can't stay anchored.
Soon we must set sail

On the last mysterious voyage
Everybody takes
Toward death.
Without my ship there,
Wish me well.

COMING INTO EIGHTY

RENASCENCE

For two years
The great cat,
Imagination,
Slept on.

Then suddenly
The other day
What had lain dormant
Woke
To a shower,
A proliferation
Of images.

My Himalayan cat
Sits on the terrace wall
Back to the sea
His blue eyes wide open

Alive to every stir of a leaf
Every wing in the air
And I recognize him
As a mage.

After long silence
An old poet
Singing again,
I am a mage myself
Joy leaps to my throat.
Glory be to God!

I WANTED POEMS
TO COME

I wanted poems to come
Running and leaping—
All they did was dream
While I was sleeping.

In the dreams I could leap
                and run
Feeling no pain
It was healing and resolution
I was given my life again.

THE O'S OF
NOVEMBER

I remember
The cold
And the somber
O's of November
No birdsong in the marsh
Not even at dawn
But only the crows
Loud and harsh.

Like the trees we are bare
And the chill on the air
Speaks of death.
They are shooting the deer.
In this time in this place
Of the dying body
It is dark now at four
We are pulled down to earth.

But the O's of November
In all times and all places
Bring the ancient rite,
Bring the snows of December.
In all the religions
All over the earth
The candles are lit
For rebirth.

DECEMBER MOON

Before going to bed
After a fall of snow
I look out on the field
Shining there in the moonlight
So calm, untouched and white
Snow silence fills my head
After I leave the window.

Hours later near dawn
When I look down again
The whole landscape has changed
The perfect surface gone
Criss-crossed and written on
Where the wild creatures ranged
While the moon rose and shone.

Why did my dog not bark?
Why did I hear no sound
There on the snow-locked ground
In the tumultuous dark?

How much can come, how much can go
When the December moon is bright,
What worlds of play we'll never know
Sleeping away the cold white night
After a fall of snow.

AS FRESH,
AS ALWAYS NEW

As fresh, as always new
As it has always been
The first fall of snow
Falls soft as in a dream
To transform the sad brown
Of late November
Into a lavish scene,
The ermine of December.

And every year we wonder,
Forlorn as we are,
What sudden clap of thunder
Or brilliance of a star
Could stop us where we are,
Could stir the roots to sense
Out of the dark once more
Rebirth of innocence.

Will it be born again,
Fresh as the first snowfall,
That love without a stain?
Who knows, who can tell?
Yet for an interval
Always the Christmas grace,
That gift beyond our will,
Makes earth a holy place.

SMALL JOYS
NEW YEAR 1990

What memory keeps fresh, frames unspoken,
I catch for you, innumerable friends.
When so much else has been destroyed or broken
These joys remain intact as the year ends,
A year of earth-grief and of bitter news,
The starving children and the burning trees,
Otters coated in oil and dolphins drowned.
Small joys keep life alive. I give you these.
They will not die, you know. They stay around.

When the long winter lingered on
And all the color stayed an ugly brown,
Suddenly snowdrops had pushed their way through
And their sharp whiteness made all new.

Early in February owls began to woo,
Their language gentle, calling, "Who? Who? Who?"
And I was lit up when an awesome bird
In the harsh cold spoke such a tender word.

The finches changed their suits early this year
From olive to bright gold, and there they were
Burbling as always, their busy flight a whir
Of yellow weaving through static air.

The daffodils in April thronged the grass
And all along the wood's edge, fabulous
To show the thousand faces of a nation,
Expected, still beyond all expectation.

Later in June, alive with silent fire,
The fireflies pulsed their firefly desire
And from the terrace I could watch the dance,
Follow their bliss. It happened only once.

Full summer brought nasturtiums in profusion
I picked and bent to drink the sweet confusion,
Yellow and orange, the fresh scent. I could
Keep summer in a bowl for days, and did.

One autumn night my cat ran to my call
And leapt five feet over the terrace wall.
A second, weightless, he flowed and did not fall
That silver splendor, princely and casual.

And last I give you murmur of waves breaking,
The sound of sleep that is a kind of waking
As the tide rises from the distant ocean
And all is still and yet all in motion.

The small joys last and even outlast earthquake.
I give you these for love—and for hope's sake.

A THOUGHT

The steamroller
That crushes a butterfly
In its path has not won
Anything
Only destroyed something.

Brute power
Is not superior
To a flower.

Through the silences,
The long empty days
You have sat beside me
Watching the finches feed,
The tremor in the leaves.
You have not left my mind.

Friendship supplied the root—
It was planted years ago—
To bring me flowers and seed
Through the long drought.

Far-flung as you are
You have seemed to sit beside me.
You have not left my mind.

Will you come in the new year?
To share the wind in the leaves
And the finches lacing the air
To savor the silence with me?
It's been a long time.

BEST FRIEND

Like two halves of an almond
We were inseparable
As children,
Made up a language
Called Oyghee
Which gave us
Our own space
And shut out the world.

Were lords
Of a summer camp
Where we entered a contest,
Decorated our canoe
As a Viking ship,
Shield-sided,
But failed to win
Because we laughed so much
The canoe capsized.

Grown up, we rarely met,
Our lives were so different.
When we did
Oyghee was spoken at once.
"How is theuta weonig?"
Hard times, illness,
Near despair,
They all poured out.

Your vision of life
Was original.
Never once did I hear you
Utter the expected
Or the usual.
That fresh look
At everything
From the mundane
To the excruciatingly private
Cost a great deal.
You could not rest in the ordinary,
The evasive
Or less than your own
Authentic truth.
Were you a genius
Who did not discover her talent?

Without writing letters
We kept in touch.
I knew I would call
If you were dying.
"Is that one dying?
This one will come."

We would talk Oyghee
One last time.
But no one told me,
And now there is no ending,
But wherever I am, you are.

THE TEACHER

I used to think
Pain was the great teacher
But after two years
Of trying to learn
Its lessons
I am hoping my teacher
Will go away
She bores me almost to death,
She is so repetitive.

The pain I meant
Is the pain of separation
The end of a love.
That lesson is never learned
And is never boring.
Only a kind of
Desolation
Like a crow cawing
In the depth of winter.
Memory is merciless.

There is a thin glass
Between me and everything I see.
The glass is pain.
How to slide it away,
Unblur my vision?

"We must rinse the eye,"
My old friend, the poet,
Used to say.
But that was in Belgium
Many years ago.

Raymond is dead
And I am in exile,
Old and ill.

My eye turns inward
To rest on three poplars
And a lost garden.
The delphinium is very blue.
The columbine, purple and white,
Trembles in the breeze
And there are tall yellow daisies.

"We must rinse the eye,"
The poet reminds me

While his wife calls out
To the children to hurry.
The garden must be watered
Before dark,
And we run for the pails.

Nothing is blurred now,
Everything is quite clear
In the poignant evening light.
An explosion of memory
Has rinsed my eye.

PALM

Veiling only a little
The bright awe of his gift,
An angel to the table
Brings fresh bread and smooth milk.
But the grave eyelids there
Gently summon to prayer,
The vision's inwardness:
—Calm, calm, be calm!
Learn the weight of the palm
Supporting its largesse.

Just as the tree is bent
Under its heavy fruit,
Just so is all assent,
Leaning on its own weight;
Lovely the slight vibration,
The threading in slow motion
As it divides the moment
And learns to arbitrate
Between earth's pulling weight
And the vast firmament.

Between the sun and shade,
Wise as a sibyl's sleep,
This judgment lightly made
Still rests upon the deep.

Patient, it never tires
Of farewells or desires,
But, centered, the palm stands.
Oh, tender noble one
Worthy to wait alone
For the gods' fertile hands.

The light gold is a murmur
Fingered by simple air
To weave a silken armor
For desert soul to wear,
Gives to the brittle wind
Shot through with shifting sand
A voice that's never done,
Is its own oracle,
A self-made miracle
When grief sings on alone.

And still itself unknowing
Between sand and the sky
While each day shines, is growing
And makes a little honey.
This sweetness of sensation
Is timeless in duration
Through days that hardly move,
Uncounted hours of presence
Secrete the living essence
And the full weight of love.

Sometimes severe endeavor
Yields only that despair
Of shadow and of languor
In spite of many a tear.
Yet do not then accuse
The tree of avarice,
Oh Gold, Authority!
Gravely the rising sap
And the eternal hope
Grow to maturity.

These seeming-empty hours,
When the whole world is gone
Send avid roots and powers
Down through the desert, down
Like myriad fine hairs
The fruitful darkness bears;
Working their way through sand
To the entrails of earth
Where sources come to birth
That the high peaks demand.

Patience, and patience,
Patience across the blue.
Each atom of your silence
Ripens the fruit in you.
The grave mercy is near,

A dove, a breath of air,
The gentlest feeling,
There where a woman leans
The light rain begins
And you are kneeling.

If now a people fall
Palm—irresistibly!
Powdered like dust to roll
With the stars in the sky!
You have not lost those hours
So lightly bear your powers
After the great outgoing;
As does the thinking one
Who spends his spirit on
The gifts of his own growing.

Translation of Valéry's "Palme"
by May Sarton, 1954

AFTER THE LONG
ENDURING
for Charles

After the long enduring,
The agony of staying alive
With AIDS inside you,

You who noticed everything
With wide open eyes,
The veins in a leaf or a wrist,
Ladybird on a grass blade at rest,
They told me, "Charles is blind."
"Blind," is what they said.

Remember the salamander
You found in the bird bath
One summer,
A vermilion streamer?
The solitary doe at dusk
Stamping and huffing
In the luscious field?
Rilke tells you
With great tenderness,
Einblick, my friend,
Inwardness, in-sight.

ELEGY
Charles Barber
1956 – 1992

So present in your absence
You will always be walking
Down the grassy path
Toward me,
Tall and smiling,
Not under the cruel spell
That has taken you away,
Blind and spent,
After the excruciating battle.

You will always be holding
My little dog tenderly
In your arms.
You will always be here with me
As long as I live,
A towering figure of love.

THE ARTIST

The drawings were abstract,
Delicate
Like Japanese calligraphy.
When the painter de Kooning
Was shown them, he said,
"Interesting.
Not done by a child, I think,
Or if so, an extraordinary child."
"The artist is an elephant, Sir,
Named Siri."

It had come about
That her keeper noticed
Her sensitive trunk
Drawing designs in the dust.
After an argument
With the head of the zoo
Who laughed at him,
The keeper himself
Brought large sheets of paper
And boxes of charcoal
And laid them at Siri's feet.
For an hour at a time
In happy concentration
The elephant created designs
Like Japanese calligraphy.

What artist's hand
As skillful
As that sensuous, sensitive trunk?

Inspired by Gary Kowalski's
The Souls of Animals,
Stillpoint Press, Walpole, NH

ALL SOULS 1991

"The children of Iraq are the most traumatized children
of war ever described."

Manchester Guardian Weekly

All Souls tonight.
What comes to me
What tears the thin wall
Between life and death?
Not my father, not my mother,
Not the great Muses,
Or beloved friends,
But the children of Iraq.
Their fifty-five thousand
Bereft souls
Cloud the dirty sky,
Will not go away.

Those still alive
Are not crying
Traumatized
By what they try to forget
The screams, the wild
Explosions, fires
The bodies of the dead,
Women, children,
Traumatized by memory
And by starvation.
They cannot sleep.

Five hundred more
Will die today
Their souls wandering
The dirty sky.

It is All Souls
And the children not crying,
All Souls
And the children dying.

We have won the war.
Who could ask for more?

Perhaps in each of us
God is dying
Because
What compassion
There may be
Is paralysed
By the overwhelming
Multiplicity
Of need.
"What can I do?"
We say.

Because we have not
Done
One simple thing
For one hungry child,
Perhaps
God is dying.

A boy shoots
His friend to death
Because he
Was teased.
He knows loss
The loss of himself,
He is terribly angry.

Perhaps God is dying
Inside of him.

A woman
Tortures her stepson,
A baby,
Tortures him horribly.
How can she do it?
Because she is furious
Against life itself,
Against the goddess
Dying inside her.

Perhaps God is dying
Because the compassion
In each of us
Finds no outlet.
We are imprisoned
By need,
Our need,
The needs of others.

Shelter the homeless
Bind up wounds.
Feed the starving
Millions of sheep.
Do something
For God's sake!
Hurry,
There isn't much time.

THE USE OF FORCE

Today
I had to force my cat,
Pierrot
Into the carrier
To take him to the Vet.

He fought so hard
I nearly fell
Holding him down,
And when at last
I managed to force
His paws under the lid
And closed it,
I began to cry.

His pride,
His sense of himself,
Noble cat,
Emperor of this domain
Had been
Brutalized.

The use of force
Exacts a formidable price
In self-loathing.
I was bruised
At the center

Where I dreamed
Tigers caught,
Women beaten
Over and over
Who always lose,
Wept bitter tears
For Pierrot
And for myself.

THE SCREAM

Strange that the rabbit,
That soft silent creature,
In the owl's talons
Suddenly screams
Like a human being
In mortal agony—
And then the horrible silence.

GUILT

Do I my life possess
Or does it possess me
A constricting dress
That fits me badly?

I am held and molded
By invisible weight
And by it enfolded
And cannot escape.

Laid down before me
Little to call my own
Of the human story
And its refrain.

Partners in a dance
They hope to touch me
Listener for once
Because they love me.

I try to pretend
They are not unknown
But I am at the end
Turned to rag and bone.

For I cannot contain
The interweaving
Of their hope and pain
And true believing.

And I cannot forget
(As if lack of funding
To pay a big debt)
My not responding.

MELANCHOLY

Crawl under the roots of a tree
No one needs you any longer.
You the destined solitary,
You can sleep away the hunger
That is tearing you apart,
Woman with an open heart.

No one's mother, no one's child
Living in unsheltered space
Be the stranger reconciled
To the absence of a face,
To the end of family,
Never able to say "we".

Woman with an open heart,
Close the valve now, dull the beat
Sleep away the stop and start.
You will find enough to eat,
Friendly trees to shelter you
And the ocean often blue.

You will comfort with a word
Others who are lost like you,
You will celebrate a bird,
Sing the song of falling snow
Become balm for every hurt,
Woman with an open heart.

FOR MY MOTHER
August 3, 1992

Once more
I summon you
Out of the past
With poignant love,
You who nourished the poet
And the lover.
I see your gray eyes
Looking out to sea
In those Rockport summers,
Keeping a distance
Within the closeness
Which was never intrusive
Opening out
Into the world.
And what I remember
Is how we laughed
Till we cried
Swept into merriment
Especially when times were hard.
And what I remember
Is how you never stopped creating
And how people sent me
Dresses you had designed
With rich embroidery
In brilliant colors
Because they could not bear

To give them away
Or cast them aside.
I summon you now
Not to think of
The ceaseless battle
With pain and ill health,
The frailty and the anguish.
No, today I remember
The creator,
The lion-hearted.

GETTING DRESSED

These days
Everything is an effort,
Getting dressed
An adventure.
I may lose my balance
Pulling on jeans,
Buttoning my shirt
A trial of patience,
Pulling on a sweater
I get lost inside it.
When I am dressed
At last
It is a small triumph
And I am rather tired
At the very start of the day.

FRIEND OR ENEMY

I can look
At my body
As an old friend
Who needs my help,
Or an enemy
Who frustrates me
In every way
With its frailty
And inability to cope.

Old friend,
I shall try
To be of comfort to you
To the end.

WANTING TO DIE

Sometimes
I want to die,
To be done with it all
At last,
Never make my bed again,
Never answer another letter
Or water the plants,
None of those efforts
I must make
Every day
To keep alive.

But then
I do not want to die.
The leaves are turning
And I must see
The scarlet and gold
One more time,
A single yellow leaf
Tumbling through
The sunlit air
One last time.

THE TIDES

I pretend
To live in the present.
Now is what I crave,
Finches at the feeder,
Sunlight on a rose.

But memory
The relentless tide
Suddenly brings alive
A forgotten moment
With such a freight
Of passionate grief in it
I cry out
Alone.

The past is Now.
The tide rises and falls.
There is no shutting it out.

LUNCH IN THE GARDEN

We sat having lunch
In the garden
Camellias in flower
And pink viburnum
Crocus, daffodils, and anemones
On the ground
Like the border of a tapestry.

And who were we?
She is 95 now
He, her lover long ago, 81
And I the poet
Who adored her, 80.

Fifty-five years ago
He sent me a telegram
"Oh, let my joys have some abiding."
We sat in the spring garden
On a chilly March day
And the joys all around us
In the air
As elusive
As the butterfly who came to rest
For a moment on the table.
Miracles do happen
When you are old.

OBIT

Next door
He played Bach
On the harpsichord.
I listened
And wrote poems.
Fellow lodgers,
We hardly
Exchanged a word.

The obit has brought me
An acute sense of loss,
Free fall
Down a nowhere shaft,
As when he told me
He was engaged
To someone else.
In Bloomsbury
Fifty-five years
Ago.

A FORTUNE

Forty-eight years ago
An Italian painter
Called Cagli
Read my fortune
With the Tarot pack.

I was thirty-four;
I had no job;
My adored muse
Had died,
Leaving me no word.

Cagli shuffled
Looked hard at the cards
He had lain before me,
And then at me
Apparently amazed.

"It will all come out
At the end," he said,
"Money, love, glory
Will all be there for you
At the very end."

Can you believe it?
Now I am eighty

The long game of solitaire
Has ended
Exactly as he said
It must.

Whom to thank?
My guardian angel,
Or my innumerable
Friends?

TO HAVE WHAT I HAVE

It was you,
Jean Dominique,
Who made me hope
To grow old,
To experience someday
The kind of wisdom,
The special laughter,
And above all the poetry
That inhabited
Your tiny frame,
You with your huge gray eyes
Hidden behind dark glasses
Most of the time.

You were not beautiful,
To me at fourteen
A very old woman,
But you were the epitome
Of glamour
In the sheer intensity
Of your being,
Unique in the universe,
An extraordinary treasure.

And so you stayed
When we became close,

As close as lovers
Who guess what the other
Feels and can express it,
From my twenty-fifth year
Until you died.

No one will ever again
Lean her head on my shoulder
And sleep a little,
Or hold my hand in a small dry hand,
Or read her poems
In an unforgettable voice,
Or take off her glasses
To blaze my heart.

Forty years later
It is very lonely here
Because I am eighty
And it was so long ago
When I wanted to be eighty
And have what I have,
And be what I am.
Oh please remind me of your laughter
I need it now,
To help me balance so much lost
Against so much won,
And rejoice.

BLISS

In the middle of the night,
My bedroom washed in moonlight
And outside
The faint hush-hushing
Of an ebbing tide,
I see Venus
Close to
The waning moon.
I hear the bubbling hoot
Of a playful owl.
Pierrot's purrs
Ripple under my hand,
And all this is bathed
In the scent of roses
By my bed
Where there are always
Books and flowers.

In the middle of the night,
The bliss of being alive!

LUXURY

My cat, Pierrot
The eloquence
Of his sleep!
Tucked under
The ample breast
His paws
Are two velvet pillows
His thick-furred boots
Stretch out
In luscious abandon,
His colors are blue-gray
And silvery white.
His purrs lightly
Embroider the air.

No emerald,
No mink muff,
No ermine vest
Could provide
The luxury
Of this cat's sleep.
How rich I am!

Becoming eighty
Might be nothing much
If I could be well,
But it feels weighty

Because I am in touch
Because I have been ill
With Heaven and with Hell,
Unbalanced on that crutch,

A place of no return
And of no mending
With a long life to burn
And its long ending.

The ender, the beginner,
The child and the old soul,
The mystic and the sinner
At eighty remain whole.

I am still whole and merry
And when all's said and done
Rejoice in my strange story,
Ardent and alone.

"What are you doing
Now the end is not far?
Remembering? Rueing?"
"No rue, my dear."

"Are you still seeding?"
"Now and then I do."
"You are frail for weeding,
And the weeds grow."

"Yes, the weeds flourish.
Too brief the hours
When I can still nourish
Poems or flowers."

"The muses have died?"
"Not died. I must be
My own muse beside
My own mystery.

And the memories move
Without warning to break
Happiness, even love
For poetry's sake."

"But what will you keep
When you can't even rhyme?"
"Sleep, my dear, sleep
And a handful of thyme."

BIRTHDAY PRESENT

I am eighty today
How can I have lived so long
Such a complexity of work, people, events
I ask myself in some dismay,
And turn to the window
To catch in my dazzled eye
A scarlet tanager
In the cherry tree.

The last time I beheld
That scarlet and black
Sumptuous bird
Was when I moved into
This house by the sea
Twenty years ago.
He flew to the flowering
Andromeda.

I have travelled so far
Through time
To arrive at this moment
Awestruck.

The complex forms of being
And a magic bird
Gathered up
Into one overwhelming
NOW!

Nothing else exists
Ecstasy and peace
Are mine forever
On this birthday.

May Sarton is the author of seventeen poetry collections, nineteen novels, eleven journals, and two children's books. But her poetry remains closest to her heart: "If I were in solitary confinement, I'd never write another novel, and probably not keep a journal, but I'd write poetry, because poems, you see, are between God and me." Sarton has taught and read her poems in colleges and universities all over the country, and holds seventeen honorary doctorate degrees. Her most recent books are *Collected Poems (1930– 1993)* and *Encore: A Journal of the Eightieth Year. May Sarton: Among the Usual Days*, edited by Susan Sherman, a portrait of May Sarton through unpublished poems, letters, and journals, was published in 1993. Sarton received the 1993 Levinson Prize from *Poetry* magazine for poems in *Coming into Eighty.*

May Sarton lives by the sea in York, Maine.